Basic Bible 101
The Old Testament Student Workbook
By Margie Smith

This worbook is designed to be used along with *Basic Bible 101 The Old Testament Teacher's Manual,* or with the podcast of Basic Bible 101 presented by Margie Smith. Reference materials, group leader assistance and answers to the questions posed here are available on line at www.basicbible101.com. Additional information about the author, ordering more workbooks, and accessing the student area of the website can be found on the last page of this workbook. Thank you for purchasing *Basic Bible 101 - The Old Testament Student Workbook.*

Disclaimer: *While we have made every effort to check the accuracy of the information contained herein, it is possible that some of the text is misquoted, contains the wrong reference, is missing some text or in any of a thousand ways is just plain wrong. Please forgive the error and let us know. We will correct these errors in the next edition of this workbook.*

Copyright @ 2003 Margaret A. Smith All rights reserved. ISBN: 978-1-304-95198-4

All scripture quotations, unless otherwise indicated, are taken from
The New International Version of the Bible.

Basic Bible 101 - The Old Testament
Table of Contents

Lesson 1	What is Basic Bible 101?	1
Lesson 2	In the Beginning	4
Lesson 3	Adam & Eve	6
Lesson 4	Noah & The Flood	8
Lesson 5	Abraham	10
Lesson 6	Issac the Promised Son	12
Lesson 7	Jacob & Esau	14
Lesson 8	Joseph	16
Lesson 9	Moses	18
Lesson 10	Israel Freed	20
Lesson 11	The 10 Commandments	22
Lesson 12	Balaam's Donkey	24
Review of Leviticus, Numbers & Deuteronomy		26
Lesson 13	Joshua	28
Lesson 14	Deborah the Judge	30
Lesson 15	Gideon	32
Lesson 16	Samson & Delilah	34
Lesson 17	Ruth	36
Lesson 18	Samuel	38
Lesson 19	King Saul	40
Lesson 20	David & Goliath	42
Lesson 21	David & Bathsheba	44
Lesson 22	King Solomon	46
Lesson 23	The Prophet Elijah	48
Lesson 24	The Prophet Elisha	50
Lesson 25	Job	52
Lesson 26	Jonah & The Whale	54
Lesson 27	Isaiah	56
Lesson 28	Jeremiah	58
Lesson 29	Daniel	60
Lesson 30	Ezekiel	62
Lesson 31	Ezra & Nehemiah	64
Lesson 32	Esther	66

Reference Materials

Basic Bible 101 - The Old Testament
Lesson 1 - What is Basic Bible 101?

Basic Bible 101 is...

1. Basic Bible 101 is a brief overview of the entire Bible, not an in-depth verse-by-verse study.

2. Basic Bible 101 is a one-year commitment to read the assigned Bible passages, answer the discussion questions, attend every session, study for the quizzes and take the final exam. You may choose to tackle the larger goal of reading the Bible completely through by following the course outline of recommended readings for each week.

3. An opportunity to:
   • Make friends
   • Share struggles and ask for prayer
   • Learn how to apply the Bible to your present situation
   • Strengthen family relationships

What can you expect each week?

In this workbook you will find all your study materials. Additionally we will be using a common version of the Bible, *NIV Student Bible (Zondervan Publishing Co)*, primarily so we will be reading the same words. Throughout the class we will be using the charts and maps included here, as well as other reference materials.

We will begin each week with a review of the previous lesson, then move into a short description of the main story for that day. Your discussion leader will ask some general discussion questions as you work through the Bible passage. Then you will have an opportunity to share your answers with the rest of your group. Finally, we will end with a concluding thought and a time for sharing prayer requests. Your discussion leader may ask for a volunteer to close in prayer.

After we finish a section you will take a quiz over those lessons, and at the end of this course you will be given a final exam. Along the way you will be given review notes and "pop" quizzes to remind you of the main points. If you are taking this course individually, via the internet, then you can check the answers to your homework on line at www.basicbible101.com.

Some Class Rules:

1. You will never be asked to read, pray out loud, answer a question or share anything. You will, however be given an opportunity to do so. Your discussion leader will simply say, "Would anyone like to read ..." Remember you will get more out of the class if you participate, and it will keep others from getting bored!

Student Notes:

_____
_____
_____
_____
_____
_____
_____
_____
_____
_____
_____

Lesson 1 - What is Basic Bible 101?

Men who brought us the Bible:

- Moses - Tablets of Stone
- Jewish Scribes - Scrolls
- Hebrew Scholars - Septuagint
- Apostles - Letters
- Christian Scribes - Dead Sea Scrolls
- Jerome under Pope Damasus - Vulgate
- John Wycliff - First English version
- Johann Gutenberg - First printing
- William Tyndale - Layman's version
- Martin Luther - Stood for the right for everyone to study the Bible
- King James I - First official public version of the Bible

Student Notes:

_____
_____
_____
_____
_____
_____
_____
_____
_____
_____
_____

2. There are NO stupid questions -- ask whatever you like. If your discussion leader doesn't know, he or she will find the answer, or you can email me at margie@basicbible101.com. If no one knows, then we'll just give the various opinions on the matter.

3. The class closes after the fourth week. The reason for this rule is because we will cover so much of the Bible so quickly that it's too difficult to make up the missed weeks.

4. Fill in the answers to these questions as you listen to the lesson presentation.

Lesson Notes

What is the Bible?
_____
_____
_____
_____

Who wrote it?
_____
_____
_____
_____

How did the Bible get into this form?
_____
_____
_____
_____

Why are there so many versions?
_____
_____
_____
_____

Why is every sentence numbered?
_____
_____

Lesson 1 - What is Basic Bible 101?

How can you be sure it's accurate?

_____

_____

_____

What's the best way to study the Bible?

_____

_____

_____

What's the homework for next week?

Genesis Chapter 1 & 2 (The Creation Story)

To read through the Old Testament: Genesis 1-2

Old Testament

The Law

History of the Israelites

Judges & Kings

The Prophets

Student Notes:

_____
_____
_____
_____
_____
_____
_____
_____
_____
_____

Basic Bible 101 - The Old Testament
Lesson 2 - In The Beginning

Homework Questions

Read: Genesis 1

1. The Bible begins with a discussion of whether or not God exists.
   True   False   (circle one)

2. What was the earth before God began creating it?
   _____
   _____

3. Have you ever experienced the grandeur of God in nature? Describe your experience:
   _____
   _____
   _____
   _____

3. List what God created on each day, according to Genesis 1:

   Day 1 _____
   Day 2 _____
   Day 3 _____
   Day 4 _____
   Day 5 _____
   Day 6 _____

4. What did God do on the 7th day? Why?
   _____
   _____

5. What surprises you the most about this account of creation?
   _____
   _____

6. Knowing that God created everything just the way he wanted it, does it change your opinion of how he created you?
   _____
   _____

Personal Notes:
   _____
   _____
   _____

To read through the Old Testament: Genesis 1-2

Student Notes:
_____
_____
_____
_____
_____
_____
_____
_____

Lesson 2 - In The Beginning

Lesson Notes

What was the light described in verse 3?
_____

How does God describe everything he creates?
_____

What did God intend for people to eat?
_____
_____

Why is it important to rest one day a week?
_____
_____

Passages describing God as creator...
Romans 1:20 *"For since the creation of the world God's invisible qualities – his eternal power and divine nature – have been clearly seen, being understood from what has been made, so that men are without excuse."*

Jeremiah 32:17 *"Ah, Sovereign Lord, you have made the heavens and the earth by your great power and outstretched arm. Nothing is too hard for you."*

Psalms 50:1 *"The Mighty One, God, the Lord, speaks and summons the earth from the rising of the sun to the place where it sets."*

Psalms 24:1 *"The earth is the Lord's, and everything in it, the world, and all who live in it; for he founded it upon the seas and established it upon the waters."*

Psalms 19:1-3 *"The heavens declare the glory of God; the skies proclaim the work of his hands. Day after day they pour forth speech; night after night they display knowledge. There is no speech or language where their voice is not heard."*

Psalms 8:3-9 *"When I consider your heavens, the work of your fingers, the moon and the stars, which you have set in place, what is man that you are mindful of him, the son of man that you care for him? You made him a little lower than the heavenly beings and crowned him with glory and honor. You made him ruler over the works of your hands; you put everything under his feet; all flocks and herds, and the beasts of the field, the birds of the air, and the fish of the sea, all that swim the paths of the sea. O Lord, our Lord, how majestic is your name in all the earth."*

For more reflections on God the creator see Job 38-41

Student Notes:
_____
_____
_____
_____
_____
_____
_____
_____
_____
_____

Basic Bible 101 - The Old Testament
Lesson 3 - Adam & Eve

The Garden of Eden could have been located between the Tigris & Euphrates rivers. See larger map on page 11.

Student Notes:

Homework Questions

Read: Genesis 2-3

1. With what did Satan tempt Eve? Why did this work?

2. What is your greatest temptation?

3. How did Adam respond to God's call? Why?

4. What were the consequences of Adam & Eve's sin?

5. What did God do to cover Adam and Eve's sin?

6. What consequences do we live with today because of their original sin?

To read through the Old Testament: Genesis 3-5

Lesson 3 - Adam & Eve

Lesson Notes

Major concepts introduced in this lesson:

Helpmate – The original marriage
Walking in the Garden – The original relationship with God
Avoiding the Two Trees – The original law
Satan as Serpent – The original tempter
Adam & Eve's Disobedience – The original sin
String of Leaves – The original cover-up
Garments of Animal Skins – The original sacrifice
Banished from the Garden – The original fall of mankind

What qualities do you see in a good marriage from Gen. 2:24-25?
_____
_____

According to James 1:13-17, what are the consequences of giving in to temptation?
_____
_____

How did Adam and Eve know they were naked?
_____
_____

Why were Adam and Eve banished from the Garden of Eden?
_____
_____

Conclusion

Sin caused man to be separated from God. Sin spoils everything – separates families, destroys confidence and trust in God, creates scars and hardships that we endure all our lives. With Adam and Eve's original sin came death, which is the fallen state we all live in.

How can we be free of our sin?
_____
_____

Where did Satan come from?

The Bible doesn't tell us much about where Satan came from, but it does give us some clues. 2 Pet. 2:4 mentions that God did not spare the angels when they sinned but cast them into hell. Apparently a rebellion occurred in heaven sometime between Genesis 1:31 and Genesis 3. Among the angels, the heavenly beings that God created to help him in his work, a leader arose who believed he was just as good as God. Isaiah seems to describe this evil one in Isaiah 14:12-15. We commonly call this rebellious head angel Satan. The book of Job gives us more insight into this devilish being in that he comes before God and harasses mankind when God permits it. Satan is referred to as the "father of lies" (John 8:44) and "the evil one" (Matt. 13:19). We know that Satan's power is limited by God. Satan and God are not equal. Eventually the Son of God, Jesus Christ, will finish his work on earth and destroy Satan once and for all (Rev. 20:1-3). In the meantime, Satan prowls among mankind with the intent to come between us and God, and eventually destroy us. (2 Pet. 5:8). Our response should be to stay close to God and resist the devil. (For a more in depth discussion see "Satan & Demons," p. 412 in *Systematic Theology* by Wayne Gruden)

Student Notes:

Basic Bible 101 - The Old Testament
Lesson 4 - Noah & the Flood

Homework Questions

Read: Genesis 6:5 through 7:5

1. What reason did God give for flooding the earth?

2. How was Noah different from the other people living at that time?

3. What did God ask Noah to do?

4. Would you have been willing to take on such a huge task?

5. How many of each "clean" animal was Noah to bring? (7:2)

6. How many days did it rain?

7. What saved Noah and his family from the flood?

8. What saves us from God's wrath?

To read through the Old Testament: Genesis 6-17

Student Notes:

Lesson 4 - Noah & the Flood

Lesson Notes

What qualities do you see in Noah?

_____

_____

How long were Noah and his family in the Ark?

_____

_____

What do the dove and the olive branch now symbolize?

_____

_____

What was Noah's first act after leaving the ark? Why?

_____

_____

What sign does God use to remind us that he will never again destroy the earth by flood?

_____

It doesn't take mankind long to again fall into sin. Why did God destroy the Tower of Babel?

_____

_____

_____

What were the consequences for people?

_____

_____

_____

Conclusion
1. Man's bent is always to evil.
2. God makes his covenant (promise) with us because he loves us.
3. Cleansing on the inside comes from sacrifice.
4. Leaving behind an altar or symbol (pile of rocks - written statement) of your agreement with God can be a great reminder.

Student Notes:

Basic Bible 101 - The Old Testament

Lesson 5 - Abraham

Homework Questions

Read: Genesis 12:1-9

1. List the promises God made to Abram (later called Abraham):

2. What did Abram have to do in return?

3. Look back in Chapter 11 verse 29-30. Why might Abram have doubted God's promises?

4. Skip forward to Chapter 15 verses 1-6. How did God's promise compare to Abram's reality?

5. What did Abram do to be considered "righteous"?

6. What do we have to do to be considered righteous? (see Galatians 5:5 and Ephesians 2:8-9)

7. Read Hebrews 11:11-12. How was Abraham's faith rewarded?

To read through the Old Testament: Genesis 18-24

Student Notes:

Lesson 5 - Abraham

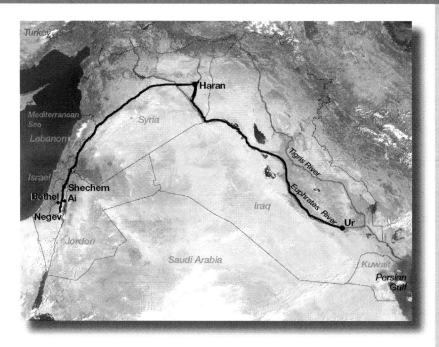

Lesson Notes

Why was God unhappy with the tower the people built?
_____
_____

Where did Abram go to escape the famine?
_____

Why did Lot and Abram separate their herds?
_____
_____

What strange vision sealed the covenant between Abram & God?
_____
_____

How did Abraham try to accomplish God's purpose on his own?
_____
_____

Conclusion
1. God calls people individually, asking them to be his own.
2. God cares more about our motives than our actions.
3. God always fulfills his promises.
4. God sees us and hears our cries.

Student Notes:

Basic Bible 101 - The Old Testament
Lesson 6 - Isaac

Homework Questions

Read: Genesis 22:1-19

1. Do you sense any hesitation in Abraham to follow God's command?

2. After God finally gave Abraham the promised heir, why do you think he put Abraham to this test?

3. Do you see any resistance in Isaac? Why didn't he run away?

4. What did Abraham call this place up on the mountain?

5. What lesson do you think Abraham learned from this experience? And Isaac?

6. If God had asked you to give up the most precious thing in your life, what would you have done?

7. What would later generations say about Abraham's experience? (see Hebrews 11:17-19)

8. How does Abraham's obedience confirm his faith? (see James 2:20-24)

To read through the Old Testament: Genesis 25-36

Student Notes:

Lesson 6 - Isaac

Lesson Notes

Who were the three strangers that showed up in front of Abraham's tent?
_____
_____

Do we have the right to question God? Can we change his mind?
_____
_____

What kind of man would give up his daughters to protect two strangers?
_____
_____

When asked to sacrifice his only son, the son of promise, what did Abraham do? Why didn't he question God?
_____
_____

How did Abraham's servant know he was choosing the right woman for Isaac?
_____
_____

How can we determine God's will?
_____
_____

Conclusion
1. God can and often does test our faith.
2. Righteousness is the result of faith.
3. If we want to know what God wants us to do we should begin by asking him.
4. God loved Issac, just like he loves you, and has provided the substitute (the lamb of God -- Jesus) for your life.

Tests for determining God's will:
1. What does the Bible say about this? (scriptures God brings to mind or through your daily devotions)
2. What do my parents, spouse, Christian mentors and small group members say about this?
3. What do circumstances seem to point toward?
4. How has God worked in my life up to this point? Is this move consistent with his previous promptings?
5. When I pray, what does God seem to be saying to me? (listen quietly and carefully – meditate on his Word if necessary)

Scriptures that may help:
Joshua 1:7-8; Eph. 5:17-6:3; All of Proverbs, Hebrews 4:12, Heb. 13:17, James 1:5-7, John 8:47). For further study on this topic see "Experiencing God" by Henry Blackaby and Claude King.

Student Notes:
_____
_____
_____
_____
_____
_____
_____
_____
_____
_____
_____

Basic Bible 101 - The Old Testament
Lesson 7 - Jacob & Esau

Homework Questions

Read: Genesis 25:21-34 and 27:1-33

1. How did Isaac and Rebekah's partial treatment of their sons affect the boys?

2. How much importance did Esau place on his birthright?

3. How important was the father's blessing to both sons?

4. Do you feel you have your father's blessing? Why or why not?

5. How has that blessing (or lack thereof) affected your life?

6. What happened to this family as a result of Rebekah and Jacob's deception? (read further in Genesis to discover the answer).

To read through the Old Testament: Genesis 37-50

Student Notes:

Lesson 7 - Jacob & Esau

Lesson Notes

What is the birthright?
_____
_____

What is the blessing?
_____
_____

What tricks did Leban play on Jacob? How did they work out in Jacob's favor?
_____
_____
_____
_____

What is the new name God gives Jacob?
_____

On Jacob's return to his childhood home, what strange event happens in the night?
_____
_____

What does Jacob insist on from the angel before he will release him?
_____

How does the reunion between Esau and Jacob turn out?
_____
_____

Conclusion
1. Don't be afraid to wrestle with God. He blesses those who overcome.
2. If you have someone in your family with whom you've struggled today is the day to settle the dispute and offer forgiveness.
3. From today's lesson you'll want to remember these Conclusion

1 - Sibling rivalry was encouraged by both parents (Rebekah and Isaac) to the destruction of the entire family.
2 - The blessing was passed down through Jacob by God's design.
3 - Two dreams show God's work in Jacob's life. God promises to bless and protect him. Jacob responds by pledging his allegiance to this God of his father. God blesses his ability to overcome the fight between right and wrong. Jacob is renamed Israel.
4 - Trickery begets trickery as Jacob is fooled into marrying the wrong woman. (Once again the consequences of sin cannot be avoided).
5 - Family healing begins with saying "I'm sorry, will you forgive me. I forgive you".

The 12 tribes of Israel - Jacob's Sons
Sons by Leah
- Reuben
- Simeon
- Levi
- Judah
- Issachar
- Zebulun

Sons by Rachael
- Joseph
- Benjamin

Sons by Bilhah
- Dan
- Naphtali

Sons by Zilpah
- Gad
- Asher

The only daughter (Leah's) was Dinah

Student Notes:
_____
_____
_____
_____
_____
_____
_____
_____
_____
_____

Basic Bible 101 - The Old Testament
Lesson 8 - Joseph

Homework Questions

Read: Genesis 37

1. Why did Joseph's brothers hate him so much?

2. What do you think Joseph's brothers thought of his dream?

3. Which brother tried to rescue Joseph, or at least spare his life?

4. Do you have brothers and/or sisters? Did you all get along well? If not, why not?

5. How did Jacob (now called Israel) react to the news about Joseph?

To find out how God used Joseph's misfortune for his ultimate good, read the rest of Genesis. What lessons can we learn from Joseph's life? Has God worked in a similar way in your life?

To read through the Old Testament: Exodus 1-6

Student Notes:

Lesson 8 - Joseph

Lesson Notes

How is the sibling rivalry between Joseph and his brothers similar to that of Jacob & Esau?

_____
_____
_____

What was Joseph's reason for not sleeping with Potipher's wife?

_____
_____

How long does Joseph sit in prison? How long after the successful dream interpretations on Pharaoh's birthday?

_____
_____

What did Joseph's dream about 7 fat cows and 7 skinny cows mean?

_____
_____
_____

When Joseph reveals himself to his brothers, what is their response?

_____
_____
_____
_____

After this story in Genesis the descendants of Jacob (Israel) remain in Egypt a long time. At first they stay willingly; then they are held captive and forced to work for the new Pharaoh as slaves. Joseph makes his sons promise to carry his body with them back to Canaan after he dies. Little did he know that would be 400 years later.

Conclusion
1. Sins are passed down from generation to generation, as we see here in the rivalry between Joseph and his brothers.
2. Just because you do the right thing doesn't mean you're going to avoid pain. Although Joseph resisted Potipher's wife, he still went to prison.
3. What Satan means for evil God uses for good in the lives of those he loves.
4. It is possible to outstay your welcome.

Student Notes:

Basic Bible 101 - The Old Testament

Lesson 9 - Moses

Homework Questions

Read: Exodus 3:1-15

1. What did God ask Moses to do before he could come closer? Why?

2. How did Moses respond when God talked to him? Why?

3. What did God want Moses to do for him?

4. What name did God give himself?

5. What did God promise Moses?

6. Where was Moses supposed to lead the people?

7. If you had seen this incredible sight, and heard God's voice, what questions would you have had for God?

To read through the Old Testament: Exodus 7-15

Student Notes:

Lesson 9 - Moses

Lesson Notes

Exodus 1 - Circumstances of Moses' childhood

- Descendants of Israel in Bondage
- Edict to kill male babies
- Moses placed in the river and adopted by Pharaoh's daughter
- Moses kills an Egyptian
- Moses flees to Midian where he lives for 40 years

When God called Moses, what signs did he give him to show Pharaoh?
_____
_____
_____

What reasons does Moses give for not using him for this assignment?
_____
_____

What was the Elders' response to Moses?
_____
_____

What was Pharaoh's response to Moses?
_____
_____

Conclusion
1. God had a purpose for Moses from birth.
2. God refines our faith through wilderness experiences.
3. God wants us to experience his presence.
4. When the task seems too great, God provides the skills and resources.
5. When facing obstacles we may experience a crisis of faith, but God is faithful.

Student Notes:
_____
_____
_____
_____
_____
_____
_____
_____
_____
_____
_____
_____

Basic Bible 101 - The Old Testament

Lesson 10 - Israel Freed

Homework Questions

Read: Exodus 14

1. What reason did God give for wanting the people to turn back and camp near the sea? (v. 3-4)

2. How did the Israelites react when they saw Pharaoh's army pursuing them?

3. What did Moses say to the people? (v. 13-14)

4. Have you ever been in a situation when you just needed the Lord to fight for you because there was nothing you could do? Explain.

5. How did God prove himself mighty to the people of Israel?

6. How has God proved himself mighty to you?

To read through the Old Testament: Exodus 16-34

Student Notes:

Lesson 10 - Israel Freed

Lesson Notes

Exodus 7-14 - Moses before Pharaoh

How could Pharaoh's magicians imitate Moses' miracles?
_____
_____

List the 10 plagues on Egypt:

_____ _____

_____ _____

_____ _____

_____ _____

_____ _____

What does it mean when the Bible says "God hardened Pharaoh's heart"?
_____
_____

What was the "Passover" and why is it still celebrated?
_____
_____
_____

How did God provide a way for the people to cross the Red Sea? What happened when Pharaoh's army tried to follow?
_____
_____

What two symbols did God use to guide the people of Israel through the desert?
_____

Conclusion
The ultimate message here is that God will make a way for his people, even when the odds are impossible – not by our might but by the Lord's. When you face an obstacle that is too great for you, a battle you can't win, remember Exodus 14:14: *"The Lord will fight for you; you need only be still."*

Exodus 14:14: *"The Lord will fight for you; you need only be still."*

Student Notes:
_____
_____
_____
_____
_____
_____
_____
_____
_____
_____
_____
_____

Basic Bible 101 © 2003 Margaret A. Smith www.basicbible101.com

Basic Bible 101 - The Old Testament
Lesson 11 - The 10 Commandments

Homework Questions

Read: Exodus 20:3-17

1. Rewrite each of the Ten Commandments in your own words. As you do so, put a star next to the ones you have kept:

_____

Now read: Exodus 32-34

2. When Moses came back down from the mountain after receiving the Ten Commandments from God, what did he find in the camp?

_____

3. What was God's punishment for the rebellion of his people?

_____

4. Why did Moses wear the veil over his face (34:33-35)?

_____

To read through the Old Testament: All of Leviticus & Numbers, but if that's too much, then just read Numbers 6-24

Student Notes:

Lesson 11 - The 10 Commandments

Lesson Notes

Exodus 15-40

How did the Israelites fare in the harsh wilderness conditions?

How did God provide for them?

How did Aaron and Hur help Moses in the war with the Amalekites? (chapter 17)

Why did God give his people "the Law"?

Why did Aaron make the golden calf?

What does Moses do with the tablets of stone that God wrote the 10 commandments on?

Conclusion
1. It's easy to grumble against God, yet He is always faithful.
2. God gave the law to protect us, but we were unable to obey the law. God's ultimate plan included a much-needed savior.
3. God forgives us and wants to be with us. His presence in our lives is obvious. Sometimes we try to cover up our diminishing closeness with God by putting on our own "veil".

Student Notes:

Basic Bible 101 - The Old Testament
Lesson 12 - Baalam's Donkey

Homework Questions

Read: Numbers 22

1. Why were the Moabites so afraid of the Israelites?

2. Was Balaam a true spokesman for God? Why or why not?

3. Why did God send the unseen angel to block Baalam's path?

4. Who finally brought the angel to Baalam's attention?

5. Do you think God cares about animals? Back up your answer.

6. What was the purpose of this experience for Baalam?

7. How can you apply this lesson to your life?

To read through the Old Testament: The rest of Numbers, all of Deuteronomy and Joshua 1-6.

Student Notes:

Lesson 12 - Baalam's Donkey

Lesson Notes

Review the summaries of Leviticus, Numbers and Deuteronomy (p. 26)

Numbers 13-14
What were the reports from the 12 spies? How many suggested moving forward into the promised land?
_____
_____

How did the people respond to the reports?
_____
_____

How did God respond to their lack of faith?
_____
_____

Once the people heard the verdict, 40 years of wandering in the wilderness, they decided to take matters into their own hands. What was the result?
_____
_____

Numbers 16 - Korah's revolt
Numbers 17 - Aaron -- the chosen high priest
Numbers 20 - Moses doesn't listen to God and now will not be able to enter the promised land
How did Moses disobey the Lord? (20:12)
_____

Numbers 21 - The Bronze Snake
What symbol in our modern society today comes from this strange story in numbers?
_____

Numbers 22-23 - Baalam's Donkey
After all his experiences, including hearing spoken words from his own donkey, what did Baalam eventually end up speaking as an oracle from God regarding the people of Israel?
_____
_____
_____

Next Week: Joshua 1-6 Entering the promised land.

Student Notes:
_____
_____
_____
_____
_____
_____
_____
_____
_____
_____
_____

Basic Bible 101 - The Old Testament
Review of Leviticus

Leviticus

The word "Leviticus" comes from the word "Levi." The tribe of Levi were the priests. This book is primarily instructions for the priests. It is also known as the book of the laws. Leviticus blends law and grace; shows how to worship God; gives laws for sacrifices, personal hygiene, relating to others, and other miscellaneous instructions. Leviticus acknowledges the separation between God and man, and therefore shows the need for a sacrifice. The reason we don't spend much time on this book is because Jesus became our ultimate sacrifice, bridging the gap between us and a holy God.

Offerings:

Burnt	– Fire symbolized God's consuming Holiness
Meal	– The gift of life was daily a symbol of God's perfection
Peace	– Thanksgiving offerings encouraged fellowship and communion with God
Sin	– Sin offerings brought about conviction and repentance
Trespass	– This offering sought forgiveness from others, was given when a sin was committed against another

Priests:

Priests were necessary intercessors. They offered sacrifices because they remained in a "clean" state. We no longer need priests to intercede on our behalf because Christ is our great High Priest (Heb. 4:16, 1 Pet. 2:5)

Feasts:

Of the Sabbath	– observed weekly
Of the Passover	– observed once a year (usually near our Easter)
Of Unleavened Bread	– observed immediately after Passover, lasted 7 days
Of First Fruits	– harvest festival
Of Pentecost	– 50 days after the feast of First Fruits
Of Trumpets	– New Years. Also symbolized gathering together those scattered
Of Atonement	– all sin was atoned for on this day. The High Priest entered the Holy of Holies (16:20) to atone for the sin of the people. Atonement means "to cover" as in "to cover the sin."
Of Tabernacles	– celebrated in the fall, this feast referred to living in tents and wandering in the wilderness, a reminder of their dependence on God.
Year of Sabbatical	– every 7th year no crops were planted. It was a year of meditation and devotion while the land rested.
Year of Jubilee	– every 50th year all the Hebrew slaves were f freed, all debt forgiven, lost land was returned to the original owner.

Student Notes:

Numbers & Deuteronomy

Leviticus, Numbers & Deuteronomy

Numbers

This is the book of wilderness wanderings, also known as the book of murmuring. Moses takes a census, organizes tribes, reinforces the laws of purity and leads the people as they face hostility from local tribes. This book introduces us to the term "Nazerite" – people who took a vow to be set apart by not cutting one's hair and not drinking anything from the vine. Included in Numbers are instructions for the tabernacle, observing the Passover, and other clarifications of the law. God continues to meet the daily needs of his people through manna, and when they complain for lack of meat, he sends quail – along with a plague! Miriam opposes Moses and gets leprosy.

In Numbers 13:26-33 the spies enter into Canaan but return with dismal reports. Only two of the spies are hopeful that they will be able to conquer the locals. When Moses declares that the Lord will require 40 years of wandering in the wilderness, they change their mind. Determined to take the land with or without God, they fail miserably and end up defeated badly.

In Numbers 16, the group following Korah rebel against Moses, insisting that all the people were holy, not just Moses and Aaron. The rebellion disappeared when these men were swallowed up in an earthquake.

God affirms Aaron as High Priest when his staff buds. Moses gets a bit overconfident, choosing to strike a rock for water instead of speak to it as the Lord had commanded. This error was punished by God's proclamation that Moses would not enter the promised land.

In Numbers 21 the people are bitten by poisonous snakes, but God has Moses raise up a bronze snake. Those who believed they would be healed and looked upon the snake were healed.

Numbers 22-24 covers the story of Balaam, whose donkey had to speak in order to bring his attention to the angel of the Lord. A second census is taken. Zelophehad's daughters gain equal inheritance rights with the men in chapter 36.

Deuteronomy

This final speech from Moses is his charge to the people of Israel. As they prepare to enter the promised land after 40 years of wandering in the wilderness, Moses reminds them of God's provision and protection these 40 years. He reminds them not to forget the Lord when things are good, but to obey all that the Lord has commanded them. He reviews the law and then passes the torch to Joshua. Moses blesses the tribes, then climbs Mt. Pisgah to see the promised land before dying. Jesus quotes Deuteronomy more than any other book in the Old Testament.

Student Notes:

Basic Bible 101 - The Old Testament
Lesson 13 - Joshua

Homework Questions

Read: Joshua 2 & 6 (or 1-6 if you have time)

1. Who protected the two spies in Jericho?
   _____

2. What reason did she give for seeking their favor?
   _____
   _____

3. What did the spies tell Rahab to do to protect her household during the invasion?
   _____
   _____

4. What report did the spies give Joshua (2:24)?
   _____
   _____

5. What strange battle plan did the Lord give to Joshua (6:2-5)?
   _____
   _____

6. What happened to the city of Jericho?
   _____
   _____

7. What happened to Rahab and her family?
   _____
   _____

8. What curse did Joshua place on this city (6:26)?
   _____
   _____

9. How do you think this victory affected the Israelites?
   _____
   _____

Read "Is a War Ever Holy?" on page 240 in your Student Bible and write some of your thoughts about war in the space below.
_____
_____
_____

To read through the Old Testament: finish Joshua and read Judges 1-5

Student Notes:

Lesson 13 - Joshua

Lesson Notes

Summary of Moses' Speech (Deuteronomy)
- How they got where they are today
- The importance of following God's commands
- Review of the law
- Blessings that come with obedience
- Curses for disobedience
- Renewal of the covenant
- Passing the leadership to Joshua
- Moses blesses the tribes

Describe the Ark of the Covenant

Joshua 4:18-24
What did Joshua have the people do with the stones from the river Jordan? Why?

Joshua 6 - The Battle
Why were the people willing to follow this crazy battle plan?

Joshua 10 - The Longest Day
How long did the sun stand still during the battle with the Amorites?

Joshua 20 - Cities of Refuge
What were the "cities of refuge"? Why were they needed?

Joshua 24 - Renewing the Covenant
At the end of the book of Joshua, what was the spiritual condition of the Israelites? (v. 24:16-24)

Key verses from Deuteronomy

4:29 - If you seek the Lord you will find him.

6:3-9 - Hear, O Israel: The Lord our God, the Lord is one... Love the Lord with all your heart, soul, mind, strength... Teach these commandments to your children.

7:16 - You must destroy the people in the land you are going, do not pity them.

7:25 - Burn their idols, do not covet the silver and gold on them, don't keep them.

8:2-5 - Remember how God led you in the desert to humble and test you... He provided for you in the desert... God disciplines you.

9:4-5 - You aren't getting this land because you are righteous, but because the people there are evil.

30:11-20 - What God commands isn't too difficult for you... I set before you life and prosperity, death and destruction, choose life.

31:6 - Be strong and courageous, God goes with you and will never leave you.

Student Notes:

Basic Bible 101 - The Old Testament
Lesson 14 - Deborah the Judge

Homework Questions

Read: Judges 4:4-24

1. Why were the Israelites conquered by the Canaanites?

2. What military advantage did the Canaanites have?

3. What did Deborah tell Barak, the military leader for Israel, to do?

4. What stipulation did Barak make before he would go into battle?

5. Who killed Sisera and how (yes, it's gruesome)?

6. What areas in your life would you consider an "idol"? Why?

7. How long was Deborah judge over Israel (5:31)?

To read through the Old Testament: Judges 6-8 and catch up on any missed readings.

Student Notes:

Lesson 14 - Deborah the Judge

Lesson Notes

Judges 1:28
What did the Israelites do with the people living in the land?

Judges 2-4
What was the result of the Israelites' failure to drive out the natives?

What is a prophetess?

What is an idol?

Who was Barak putting his trust in?

What was the significance of God allowing a woman to kill Sisera?

Conclusion
1. We all have "gods" that draw our attention away from God and must be destroyed.
2. Deborah was a wise judge because she courageously acted on what God promised.
3. The peace in Israel was always dependent upon the spiritual condition of the people.

Student Notes:

Basic Bible 101 - The Old Testament
Lesson 15 - Gideon

Homework Questions

Read: Judges 6

1. Why were the Israelites conquered by the Midianites?

2. Where was Gideon when the angel appeared to him (v. 11)?

3. What did the angel call Gideon (v. 12)?

4. What did Gideon call the alter where he sacrificed to the Lord (v. 24)?

5. When Gideon was uncertain about his circumstances, what did he ask God to do (v. 36-40)?

6. Is it wise to ask God for a sign to verify his will? (see Matt. 4:7)

7. Think of some ways you can verify what God is asking you to do in your life without violating Matt. 4:7. (See "Tests for Determining God's Will" p. 13)

To read through the Old Testament: Judges 9-16.

Student Notes:

Lesson 15 - Gideon

Lesson Notes

Judges 6-7

What do you think of Gideon's response to the angel? Did he recognize it was an angel?

What was the response of the townsmen to Gideon's act of tearing down the Asherah pole?

How does Joash's response quiet the crowd?

What military strategy does the Lord reveal to Gideon?

How did this tactic work?

How did overhearing the conversation between two Midianites encourage Gideon?

Conclusion

1. It's risky asking God for a sign, but God will show you his presence if you ask him.
2. God exercises our faith by putting us in seemingly impossible situations.
3. When He asks us to do impossible things, He will protect us and make us victorious.

Student Notes:

Basic Bible 101 - The Old Testament
Lesson 16 - Samson & Delilah

Homework Questions

Read: Judges 16

1. What were the requirements of a Nazarite (Numbers 6)?

2. Did Delilah really care about Samson?

3. What was the first way to subdue his strength that Samson told Delilah? Did this work?

4. How does the second explanation he gives get even closer to the truth?

5. If you had been Samson, would you have given Delilah a third chance? Why did Samson tell Delilah the truth about his strength?

6. What was Samson's eventual downfall -- his love for Delilah? His overconfidence? His stupidity?

7. How can you be sure that you are relying on God's strength and not your own?

To read through the Old Testament: Finish Judges. Read the book of Ruth.

Student Notes:

Lesson 16 - Samson & Delilah

Lesson Notes

Judges 13
What was Monoah's response to his wife's story about an angel?

_____
_____

Judges 14
Did Samson respect his parents?

_____
_____

Why did Samson insist on marrying against God's laws when God had given him such a gift?

_____
_____

What purpose did Samson's act of revenge on the Philistines serve in freeing the Israelites from these captors?

_____
_____

Judges 16
After Samson had been judge for 20 years, why did he go looking for trouble with the Philistines?

_____
_____

How did God use this foolish man for His glory?

_____
_____

Conclusion
1. When you think your strength lies in your own person, think again.
2. Watch the deceitfulness of Satan – don't give him an inch! He sneaks up on us so sweetly, persists to the point of eroding our resolve, then attacks.
3. Our life purpose may call us to give up certain things, forsake our own wants and follow a very difficult path, but God goes with us.
4. God uses even the foolish for His ultimate purpose.

Student Notes:

Basic Bible 101 - The Old Testament
Lesson 17 - Ruth

Homework Questions

Read: Ruth

1. Why did Naomi want her two daughters-in law to turn back?

2. What name does Naomi ask the town folks to call her and why?

3. How does Naomi react to Ruth's report about gleaning in Boaz's field? Why? (2:20)

4. Do you think Ruth's boldness is sneaking under Boaz's blanket was appropriate? Why or why not?

5. How does Naomi's even closer relative feel about "adopting" Naomi & Ruth? (4:6)

Read the call out in your Student Bible on page 286 about Ruth. Answer the question posed there: Do you find it hard to accept and admire those who come from outside your group (race, faith, etc.)?

To read through the Old Testament: 1 Samuel 1-8

Student Notes:

Lesson Notes

Ruth

What forced Naomi to return to Israel?

What is Ruth's attitude toward Naomi's faith?

What forced Ruth to glean left-over wheat in the field of a stranger?

How did God take care of Ruth and Naomi?

What is a "kinsmen-redeemer"?

Why did Boaz have to seek permission to take in Naomi & Ruth from the town elders?

How is what happened to Naomi & Ruth similar to what happened to us when we placed our faith in Jesus?

Note the linage at the end of Chapter 4. Ruth is King David's grandmother.

Conclusion

1. When you feel totally helples, remember God can and will provide for you.
2. Christ became our "redeemer" just as Boaz was to Ruth and Naomi. He bought us back.
3. It's not who you are but whose you are that matters in God's eyes.

Student Notes:

Basic Bible 101 - The Old Testament
Lesson 18 - Samuel

Homework Questions

Read: 1 Samuel 3:1-19

1. Who did Samuel think was calling him?

2. What message did God give young Samuel?

3. How did Eli react to the message?

4. Have you ever experienced a similar situation, when you felt God was speaking to you?

5. How did you know it was God?

6. Why was God going to punish Eli?

7. What do you think verse 19 means "He let none of his words fall to the ground."

To read through the Old Testament: Read 1 Samuel 9-16

Student Notes:

Lesson 18 - Samuel

Lesson Notes

1 Samuel 1
What did Hannah ask of God and why?

What did the priest Eli think was wrong with Hannah?

1 Samuel 2
What does it mean to "treat the Lord's offering with contempt"?

What prophecy does God give to Eli regarding his sons?

1 Samuel 4-5
What happens to the Philistines while they are in possession of the Ark of the Covenant?

How do they eventually dispose of it?

1 Samuel 6-7
What does the word "Ebenezer" mean?

Meditate on the ways God has turned your symptoms of sin into rocks that remind you of God's faithfulness.

Conclusion
1. Just as with Hannah, our completeness comes from God.
2. When the symptoms of sin show themselves, look for the root cause. We have only to ask God for forgiveness. His forgiveness is complete.
3. Turn your "tumor," or symptom of sin, into an Ebenezer, your "stone of help" that will remind you how far God has already brought you.

Student Notes:

Basic Bible 101 - The Old Testament
Lesson 19 - King Saul

Homework Questions

Read: 1 Sam. 16:6-13

1. Who was the first king of Israel?

2. Where does God look to evaluate the worth of a person (v.7)?

3. Why was this confusing for Samuel?

4. Who does God lead Samuel to anoint as future king?

5. What characteristics of a shepherd would help make one a good king?

6. What happened to David when Samuel anointed him?

7. Look forward to verse 14 -- What happened to Saul?

8. Have you felt the presence or the absence of God's spirit? What does it feel like?

To read through the Old Testament: 1 Samuel 17-24.
For another version of past events, read 1 Chronicles 1-10

Student Notes:

Lesson 19 - King Saul

Lesson Notes

1 Samuel 8
Why was Samuel so against a king?

Describe Saul when Samuel met him?

1 Samuel 13-15
Why did Saul decide not to wait on Samuel?

What additional sin against God does Saul commit in Chapter 15?

What does God value more than sacrifice (15:22)?

Conclusion
1. It's not our own wisdom, but God's will we should follow.
2. It's not our sacrifice, but our obedience He seeks.
3. It's not our outward characteristics, but our heart He values.

Student Notes:

Basic Bible 101 - The Old Testament
Lesson 20 - David & Goliath

Homework Questions

Read: 1 Samuel 17

1. Why was Goliath so intimidating to Saul and his army?
   _____

2. Did Goliath's challenge (a one-on-one battle versus a full scale war) make sense?
   _____

3. What was David doing to help Saul's army at the beginning of the war (v. 17-19)?
   _____

4. What question did David ask the soldiers that got him in such hot water with his brothers (v.26)?
   _____

5. When Saul heard of David's willingness to fight Goliath, how did he offer to help David succeed? Did this idea work?
   _____
   _____

6. What factors helped David win the battle?
   _____

7. How did the rest of the Philistine army react to Goliath's demise?
   _____

8. When they returned home, what caused Saul to be so jealous of David?
   _____
   _____

9. Are you facing any great fear or danger about which God is telling you to rely only on him?
   _____
   _____

To read through the Old Testament: Finish 1 Samuel, then read 2 Samuel Chapters 1-12.
Read David's writings: Psalms

Student Notes:

Lesson 20 - King David

Lesson Notes

1 Samuel 16-17

At the end of chapter 16 Saul hires David to play the harp for him. Why?
_____

What reward did David receive for slaying Goliath?
_____

Saul's son Jonathan and David become great friends. How does Jonathan help spare David's life? (Chpt. 19-20)
_____
_____

David becomes an outlaw, living among the Philistines. He has ample opportunities to kill Saul. Why doesn't he?
_____

In Chapter 25, how does Abigail rectify the mistake her husband has made? Does this work?
_____
_____

What eventually happens to Nabal, Abigail's husband? What happens to Abigail?
_____
_____

Why does Saul visit the Witch of Endor? Was this against God's law? What was the outcome for Saul?
_____
_____

Conclusion
1. Giants are not to be feared if the Lord is with you.
2. Reverence for those in authority is well documented in the Bible.
3. A wise woman's quick actions saved her entire household, so God removed her from a miserable marriage, blessing her with a loving husband.
4. It's not a good idea to dabble in witchcraft!

Student Notes:
_____
_____
_____
_____
_____
_____
_____
_____
_____
_____
_____
_____

Basic Bible 101 - The Old Testament
Lesson 21 - David & Bathsheba

Homework Questions

Read: 2 Samuel 11-12

1. What was the first thing that attracted David to Bathsheba?

2. What was David's first atempt at covering up the fact that he had slept with Bathsheba?

3. When that didn't work, what did he do next?

4. When it was obvious that Uriah was not going to spend the night with his wife, what did David do?

5. Who finally confronted David with his sin and how did he do it?

6. What was David's response?

7. Who has God brought into your life to tell you the truth, painful as it may be?

To read through the Old Testament: Finish 2 Samuel & 1 Kings 1-11
For another version of these events, read 1 Chronicles 11-29
Read Solomon's writings: Proverbs, Song of Songs & Ecclesiastes

Student Notes:

Lesson 21 - David & Bathsheba

Lesson Notes

2 Samuel

After running away from Saul for years, how does David respond when he hears of Saul's death?

_____
_____
_____

Why is Michael, his wife, so critical of his dancing before the Lord?

_____
_____
_____

What were the consequences of David's sin with Bathsheba?

_____
_____
_____
_____

In Psalms 51 David pours out his heart before God seeking forgiveness. Does God forgive him? (See Psalms 139)

_____
_____

Although his first son with Bathsheba dies, what becomes of the second son they have together?

_____
_____
_____

Conclusion
1. David loved God, yet he sinned.
2. Like us, his natural tendency was to cover up sin, but God wants us to confess right away.
3. Sin has consequences, sometimes beyond just our lifetime.
4. God knows everything about us but loves us anyway. He always forgives.
5. Spend some time in the Psalms!

Student Notes:

_____
_____
_____
_____
_____
_____
_____
_____
_____
_____

Basic Bible 101 - The Old Testament
Lesson 22 - King Solomon

Homework Questions

Read: 1 Kings 3:4-28

1. What did God say to Solomon in a dream (v.5)?

2. What did Solomon ask for (v.9)?

3. Did God agree to give this to Solomon (v.11)?

4. In the story of the two prostitutes, why would any woman agree to "divide" a baby, even if it wasn't hers?

5. How did Solomon's ruling affect the people (v. 28)?

6. How is the wisdom of God different from human wisdom? (see 1 Corinthians 1:19-31)

7. In light of the 1 Corinthians passage, how can we become wise?

Solomon wrote the book of Proverbs, Song of Solomon and Ecclesiastes. Spend some time reading from each of these books and write your initial impressions.

To read through the Old Testament: Finish 1 Kings
For another version of these events read 2 Chronicles 1-9

Student Notes:

Lesson 22 - King Solomon

Lesson Notes

1 Kings 10

Where did Solomon get all the money needed for building the temple?

_____

_____

Notice the care and detail that went into building the temple. What are some details that seem extravagant?

_____

_____

When it was finished, how did the people celebrate?

_____

_____

_____

What was the problem with Solomon marrying foreign women?

_____

_____

What happened to Israel after Solomon's death?

_____

_____

Conclusion
1. He wrote Proverbs, Ecclesiastes and Song of Solomon.
2. He was very wise, had international influence and built the temple.
3. He married many women, some foreigners, and was lured into idol worship.
4. He was the last king to rule over a united Israel.

United Israel: The Kings	Prophets at that Time
Saul	Samuel
David	Nathan
Solomon	

Divided Israel: The Kings of the Northern Kingdom

King	Prophet
Jeroboam 1 *(22 years)*	
Nadab *(2 years)*	
Baasha *(24 years)*	
Elah *(2 years)*	
Zimri *(7 days)*	
Omri *(12 years)*	
Ahab *(22 years)*	Elijah
Ahaziah *(2 years)*	"
Joram *(12 years)*	"
Jehu *(28 years)*	Elisha
Jehoahaz *(17 years)*	"
Jehoash *(16 years)*	"
Jeroboam II *(41 years)*	Jonah, Amos
Zechariah *(6 months)*	
Shallum *(1 month)*	
Menahem *(10 years)*	Hosea
Pekahiah *(2 years)*	"
Pekah *(20 years)*	"
Hosea *(9 years)*	"

The Kings of Judah
(Southern Kingdom)

King	Prophet
Rehoboam *(17 years)*	
Abijah *(3 years)*	
Asa *(41 years)*	
Jehoshaphat *(25 years)*	
Jehoram *(8 years)*	
Ahaziah *(1 year)*	
Athaliah *(7 years)*	
Joash *(40 years)*	
Amaziah *(29 years)*	
Azariah (Uzaiah) *(52 years)*	
Jotham *(16 years)*	Isaiah, Micah
Ahaz *(16 years)*	" "
Hezekiah *(29 years)*	" "
Manasseh *(55 years)*	
Amon *(2 years)*	Nahum, Zephaniah,
Josiah *(31 years)*	Jeremiah, Obadiah
Jehoahaz *(3 months)*	" Habakkuk
Jehoiakim *(11 years)*	"
Jehoiachin *(3 months)*	"
Zedekiah *(11 years)*	"

Exiled in Babylon	Ezekiel, Daniel
	Zechariah
	Haggai
	Malachi

Basic Bible 101 - The Old Testament
Lesson 23 - The Prophet Elijah

Homework Questions

Read: 1 Kings 18

1. Who was Obadiah and how did he live out his faith?

2. Why was Obadiah afraid to tell King Ahab that Elijah was in the country?

3. What does King Ahab think of Elijah?

4. What challenge did Elijah give the people?

5. How did Elijah "rub it in" to the prophets of Baal?

6. What was the result of the big showdown on Mt. Carmel?

7. If you had been in the audience that day, would you have believed in Elijah's God? Does God reveal himself in similar ways today?

To read through the Old Testament: 2 Kings
For another version of past events read 2 Chronicles 10-25

Student Notes:

Lesson 23 - The Prophet Elijah

Lesson Notes

1 Kings 14-19

After the nation of Israel split apart, who ruled which tribes?

_____

_____

List the kings of Israel (the northern tribes):

_____

_____

_____

List the kings of Judah (the southern tribes):

_____

_____

_____

Elijah was a prophet to which kings?

_____

List some of the miracles Elijah did?

_____

_____

How did God show Elijah his unfailing love, and encourage him when he was so depressed (Chpt. 19)? How did God speak to him?

_____

_____

_____

Conclusion
1. God can use you in powerful ways, let him.
2. When you're discouraged you may need rest, food and encouragement.
3. Ask God to show you those who are on your side.
4. God sometimes speaks in a still, small voice.

Student Notes:

Basic Bible 101 - The Old Testament
Lesson 24 - The Prophet Elisha

Homework Questions

Read: 2 Kings 4:1-37

1. What instructions did Elisha give the widow?

2. Why did Elisha always stay with the same couple when he went to Shunem?

3. How did Elisha bless this couple?

4. How did the Shunammite woman prove her faith in Elisha's God?

5. Sometimes we suffer so many disappointments that we are afraid to hope for anything good. Have you ever hoped for something just to have all hopes die? How did the experience increase your faith?

Student Notes:

To read through the Old Testament: Job (42 chapters)
Begin reading the books from the minor prophets and continue as you can until you've finished all of them:

- ❏ Hosea
- ❏ Joel
- ❏ Amos
- ❏ Obadiah
- ❏ Micah
- ❏ Nahum
- ❏ Habakkuk
- ❏ Zephaniah
- ❏ Haggai
- ❏ Zechariah
- ❏ Malachi

Lesson 24 - The Prophet Elisha

Lesson Notes

1 Kings 19:19-21

What did Elijah demand of Elisha in order to prove his total dependence on God?

_____

2 Kings 2

How did Elijah die, and who was there with him?

_____

2 Kings 3-5
List some of Elisha's miracles:
_____
_____

2 Kings 6

What did Elisha's servant see when he looked up at the hills? How did Elisha's prayers turn the tide for the Israelites in their war with Aram?

_____
_____
_____

Conclusion
1. Following God means killing the oxen, burning the plow and not turning back.
2. God sometimes brings about the apparent "death" of a vision in order that we might fully trust him.
3. In times of trouble, pray for vision (God will show you his support) and pray that the enemy will be blinded.

Student Notes:

Basic Bible 101 - The Old Testament
Lesson 25 - Job

Homework Questions

Read: Job 1

1. Was Job a Godly man? How can you tell?

2. What is God's opinion of Job? (v. 8)

3. What does Satan do to test Job's faith?

4. How does Job respond to all the bad news?

5. If you had experienced similar hardships, how would you react?

6. What good comes from having our faith tested?

7. Over the next several chapters Job's friends try to comfort him, insisting that he must have some hidden sin to deserve such hardship from God. Job himself begins to question God's justice. Read Job 38-41 and describe God's answer to Job.

8. Does this change your attitude toward God?

To read through the Old Testament: Jonah 1-4
Continue reading the other minor prophets as listed on page 50

Student Notes:

Lesson 25 - Job

Lesson Notes

Job 1 - God's response to Satan

Job 1 - Satan's response to God

Job 1 - Job's response to God's hand

Job 2 - Satan's response to Job's faith

Job 2 - God's response to Satan's challenge

Job 2 - Job's wife's response to Job's faith

Job 3-22 - Job's friends response to Job's circumstances and Job's response to his friends

Job 23+ Job questions God as does his friends

Job 38 - God's response to Job and his friends

Job 42 - Job's response back to God

Conclusion
1. When bad things happen, God is on our side.
2. Even Godly friends can give poor advice. Trust your <u>personal relationship</u> with God and let God teach you the truth.

Student Notes:

Basic Bible 101 - The Old Testament
Lesson 25 - Jonah & The Whale

Homework Questions

Read: Jonah 1

1. Why did God want Jonah to travel to Nineveh?
   _____

2. What did Jonah do instead?
   _____

3. How did the crew on the ship determine who to throw overboard?
   _____

4. Where did Jonah end up? _____

Read: Jonah 2

5. Describe Jonah's change of heart:
   _____
   _____
   _____

Read: Jonah 3

6. How does the city of Nineveh react to Jonah's preaching?
   _____
   _____

7. Does this surprise you?
   _____

8. How does God respond to the pleas of the people?
   _____

9. Does it surprise you the way God works with sinful people?
   _____

To read through the Old Testament: All of Isaiah
For more details about the kings of Israel read 2 Chronicles 26-36

Student Notes:

Lesson 26 - Jonah & the Whale

Lesson Notes

In 722 BC Assyria conquered Israel. The capital of Assyria, Nineveh, was 500 miles east of Joppa.

Why did Jonah want to avoid going to Nineveh?

_____
_____

After his experience in the whale, what is his attitude toward the Assyrians?

_____
_____
_____

How does Jonah respond when the people repent and seek God's forgiveness?

_____
_____

Why is Jonah angry with God? Is this anger justified?

_____
_____
_____
_____

Assyria plays a key role in Israel's future as we'll see next week.

Conclusion
1. You can run, but you can't hide from God. He will work his purpose in your life, you can either willingly obey, or learn the hard way.
2. God loves people more than anything. He will use us to touch the lives of others if we let him.

Student Notes:

Basic Bible 101 - The Old Testament
Lesson 27 - Isaiah

Homework Questions

Read: Isaiah 6

1. What was Isaiah's emotional state during this encounter with God?

2. How did Isaiah's attitude change after his sin had been atoned for and his guilt removed?

3. What message was Isaiah to give to the people?

4. Will all of the Israelite people be wiped out?

Read: Isaiah 53

5. Who is Isaiah describing?

Spend some time reading other passages from Isaiah (see sidebar). Record your thoughts about these passages here.

To read through the Old Testament: Jeremiah & Lamentations

Key Verses in Isaiah
Isa. 6:1-13
Isa. 7:10-14
Isa. 9:1-9
Isa. 40:1-5, 18-26
Isa. 53

Student Notes:

Lesson 27 - Isaiah

Lesson Notes

"Isaiah" means "Jehovah saves". Isaiah prophesied to these kings of Judah:

Azariah (also called Uzziah)
Jotham
Ahaz (purchased an alliance with Assyria)
Hezekiah (cleansed the temple. Reformed Judah for the good.
  God extended his life 15 years)

It is very difficult to separate which prophesies were for Judah at that time, and which were far into the future -- after Israel returns from exile. Some of these prophesies seem to foretell the birth and death of Christ. Others talk of his triumphant return.

2 Kings 19 talks about Isaiah's influence with King Hezekiah.

2 Kings 20 - Isaiah speaks to King Hezekiah about his illness
What does Isaiah tell him will happen?

_____

How does Hezekiah respond?

_____

What is the outcome of Hezekiah's prayer?

_____

Other prophets during Isaiah's time:

Micah (in Judah)
Hosea (in Israel up until Israel is taken over by Assyria
  about 715 BC)

Conclusion
1. The Bible is relevant today, just as it was then.
2. God revealed himself through the words of the prophets.
3. God *has* fulfilled and *still* fulfills his promises.

Student Notes:

Basic Bible 101 - The Old Testament
Lesson 27 - Jeremiah

Homework Questions

Read: Jeremiah 1

1. How does Jeremiah's encounter with God compare to Isaiah's?

2. How is the message Jeremiah was to preach similar to the one Isaiah preached?

3. Have you ever experienced a similar sense of deep conviction over sin, or an uncertainty that you were worthy of being used by God?

4. What promise does God make to Jeremiah that encourages him to be strong?

To read through the Old Testament: Daniel

Student Notes:

Lesson 27 - Jeremiah

Lesson Notes

Kings of Judah Jeremiah preached to:
Josiah (king at age 8, carried out extensive religious reforms,
    removed idols, but unwisely took on Egypt and lost)
Jehoahaz (only the king for 3 months - carried off by Pharaoh)
Jehoiakim (puppet of Egypt, tried to have Jeremiah put to death)
Jehoiachin (carried away by Babylon after 3 months)
Zedekiah (last king of Judah before being overtaken by Babylon)

What strange props did Jeremiah use to reinforce his message?

_____

_____

Why is Jeremiah known as the weeping prophet?

_____

_____

_____

Almost every message from Jeremiah is a negative one. In the end his prophesy about Babylon taking over Judah is more than they can take. False prophets rise up to counter Jeremiah's prophesy, but they are wrong. Jeremiah clearly states that Judah will serve King Nebuchadnezzar. After Nebuchadnezzar overtakes Judah he carries off all the nobility of Judah, the army, artists and craftsmen. One of the people carried off is Daniel, who we will learn about next week.

Other prophets during Jeremiah's time:
Zephaniah
Nahum
Habakkuk
Daniel
Ezekiel

Key Verses in Jeremiah
Jer. 3:6-10
Jer. 23:3-8
Jer. 36:1-26
Lamentations (also written by Jeremiah)

Conclusion
Following God's call means giving up some of our own comforts and desires. In return we receive God's presence, his word and his purpose in our life. Ask yourself if you are willing to follow God, no matter what. Pray that you will be willing.

Student Notes:

Basic Bible 101 - The Old Testament
Lesson 29 - Daniel

Homework Questions

Read: Daniel 1-3

After Israel is conquered by Babylon most of the people are carried off to Babylon as slaves. As one of the princes of Israel, Daniel and some of his friends were given special status and considered "advisors" to the king.

1. How does the chief official respond to Daniel's request to eat only healthy food?

2. When the guard agrees to let Daniel try his special diet for 10 days, what is the result?

3. How did God bless Daniel and his three friends? (1:17-20)

4. How does God rescue Daniel and his three friends when the king decides to put all the "wise" men to death? (2:12-19)

5. What other Bible character was able to interpret dreams? (Gen. 40)

6. What happens to Daniel's three friends when they refuse to bow down to the idol of King Nebuchadnezzar?

7. How does God protect them?

8. Who is the fourth man in the furnace?

To read through the Old Testament: Ezekiel

Student Notes:

Lesson Notes

Daniel 4
What horrible dream interpretation did Daniel have to give to Nebuchadnezzar in chapter 4?

_____

_____

When the interpretation came true, and Nebuchadnezzar had roamed around like a crazy man for a year, what was his response toward God?

_____

_____

Daniel 5
What was the writing on the wall? What did it mean?

_____

_____

What country conquered Babylon during Daniel's lifetime?

_____

Daniel 6
How did Daniel end up in a den of lions?

_____

_____

What did God do to protect him?

_____

What impact did this experience have on the Mede King Darius?

_____

_____

The end of the book of Daniel is full of mysterious prophesies that are very difficult to decipher. It is true that some echo passages in Revelations, so they may refer to the end times. Others refer to kingdoms that rise and fall during the end of the Old Testament.

Conclusion
1. We have authorities: bosses, the government, police, pastors, parents, etc.
2. God calls us to obey the authorities he places over us, but only to the point where our convictions are at risk.
3. When asked to violate God's law our loyalty must be to God first.

Student Notes:

Basic Bible 101 - The Old Testament
Lesson 30 - Ezekiel

Homework Questions

Read: Ezekiel 2 & 3

1. Where did God tell Ezekiel he was sending him? Why?

2. Would Ezekiel be responsible for whether they listened or not?

3. Would he be held responsible if he failed to warn Israel?

Read: Ezekiel 37:1-14

4. In this chapter, who is Ezekiel preaching to?

5. What is the result of his words?

6. What did the dry bones represent?

7. What hope do you find for your life in verses 12-14?

8. Think of a time in your life when all hope was gone. What turned things around for you?

To read through the Old Testament: Ezra & Nehemiah

Student Notes:

Lesson 30 - Ezekiel

Lesson Notes

From seven years before the fall of Jerusalem to 13 years into the exile in Babylon, Ezekiel prophesied to the Jewish nation through his unusual visions. Like Jeremiah, he used strange behavior to draw attention to the message of God.

Ezekiel 2-3

What was written on the scroll that Ezekiel had to eat?

_____

What did God say was the reason Israel was unwilling to listen to his words?

_____

Much of Ezekiel contains picture images of what has happened, or will happen to Israel. List some of them here:

_____
_____

Ezekiel 37

Who were the dry bones?

_____

Who brought them to life again?

_____

Where will the Lord lead them?

_____

Ezekiel spends several chapters describing the new temple. Why was it so important for Israel to rebuild the temple? (clue - read the last verse of chapter 48).

_____
_____

Conclusion
1. God can bring new life to old bones, to sinful people.
2. Be prepared, study and know God's word so you'll know what's coming.

Student Notes:

Basic Bible 101 - The Old Testament
Lesson 31 - Ezra & Nehemiah

Homework Questions

Read: Nehemiah 1- 2:9

After Israel had been carried off to Babylon, Babylon was conquered by Assyria. Then, the Medes and Persians joined forces and conquered the land. Some of the Israelites were allowed to return to their own country. The slow, painful process of rebuilding began under Ezra the priest. Now Nehemiah hears of their progress.

1. What is Nehemiah's response to what he hears?

2. What does Nehemiah ask of the Lord?

3. How does Nehemiah's relationship with the king give him the unique opportunity to make his request?

4. How does Nehemiah feel about asking the king for permission to return to Israel? (v. 2)

5. How does the king respond to Nehemiah's request?

6. Obviously Nehemiah had spent some time in preparing what he would say to the king. What other request does Nehemiah make of the king? (v. 7-8)

7. Why do you think these "letters of introduction" were so important?

8. Have you ever prayed and fasted over a major issue? What was the outcome?

To read through the Old Testament: Esther. Finish any other missed readings and begin your review for the final.

Student Notes:

Lesson 31 - Ezra & Nehemiah

Lesson Notes

Ezra 1-10

The Israelite exiles return to Israel, begin rebuilding the temple and celebrate the Passover. A revival breaks out and the people turn to the Lord. Unfortunately the progress is stalled because of local opposition.

Nehemiah 1-2

After receiving permission to return to Israel and continue the rebuilding process Nehemiah prepares for the trip.

What's the first problem Nehemiah encounters? (2:17-20)

_____

Nehemiah 4-5

Facing military opposition, how does Nehemiah respond?

_____

As the people grow discouraged, what tactics does Nehemiah use to keep them motivated?

_____

Finally, as the wall is about to be completed, Nehemiah's critics plot to kill him. But he does not run away. He faces the threat with a faith that God will protect him. The Lord does protect him and in Chapter 7 the wall is finished. The people gather for the dedication ceremony in Chapter 8 and Ezra reads from the word of God.

Nehemiah 8

Why were the people crying as they heard the Word of God read? (v.8-9)

_____

Conclusion

1. God will give you the strength to do what He calls you to.
2. Use Nehemiah's leadership principles in your job, in your family:
    - Face Criticism with Faith.
    - Face Opposition with Prayer - Post a Guard
    - Face Discouragement with Reminders of Who You're Fighting For
    - Face Oppression with An Appeal
    - Face Guilt with Grace

Student Notes:

Basic Bible 101 - The Old Testament
Lesson 32 - Esther

Homework

Read Esther 1-2

1. What is your initial impression of King Xerxes?

2. What relation is Esther (Hadassah) to Mordecai? (2:7)

3, How long did Esther undergo beauty treatments before she was finally presented to the king?

4. How does Esther show wisdom in preparing to visit the king? (2:15)

5. What was the king's reaction to Esther?

Though she lived much of her life as an orphan, God raised Esther to a place of prominence for a special purpose. Read the rest of the book to discover what that purpose was.

6. How has God used special (perhaps unfortunate) circumstances in your past to accomplish his purpose?

Homework for next week: Review the handout to prepare for the final! You can obtain this handout at http://www.basicbible101.com/students

Student Notes:

Lesson 32 - Esther

Lesson Notes

1. What happened to the King's first wife?
   _____
   _____

2. In what country does this story take place?
   _____

3. Who was Haman and what was his relationship with the king?
   _____
   _____
   _____

4. How did Esther's influence save her people?
   _____
   _____
   _____
   _____

5. How is Esther's story similar to Joseph's (Genesis 37-45)?
   _____
   _____
   _____
   _____

Conclusion
God can use any circumstance in our lives for his good if we are willing to let him.

Student Notes:

Summary of The Minor Prophets

Prophets of the Southern Kingdom - Judah

Obadiah - 853 BC or 605 BC
God's judgment of proud Edom and restoration of Israel. (Obadiah was a contemporary of Elisha or Jeremiah)

Micah - 750 - 722 BC
A just and merciful God delivers his people from darkness. The lives of God's people should reflect God's standards. Micah prophesied during the reigns of Jotham, Ahaz and Hezekiah.

Nahum - 623 - 612 BC
The Lord's judgment of Nineveh -- years after Jonah.

Zephaniah - 715 - 686 BC
Prophesied during the reign of Josiah. He speaks of the coming day of the Lord. (Zephaniah was an older contemporary of Jeremiah.)

Habakkuk - 610 - 605 BC
Faith triumphs over doubt. Habakkuk wrestles with a problem that faces every age: Why does God seem inactive in the face of evil and injustice?

Prophets of the Northern Kingdom - Israel

Amos - 750 BC
God's judgment on injustice. (Prophesied during Uzziah and Jeroboam II) Amos calls for social justice as the foundation for true respect for God.

Hosea - 793 - 753 BC
God's undying love for his people. Hosea married a prostitute and she bears children. Hosea said that despite Israel's unfaithfulness, God remains faithful.

Prophets of the Restoration

Zachariah - 520 - 490 BC
Rebuilding the temple and the nation of Judah; the Lord's return.

Haggai - 520 BC
Rebuilding for results -- the blessing is in the doing. His prophesies got the people moving to rebuild the temple.

Joel - 539 - 331 BC
Call to repentance. A plague of locusts indicates the Day of the Lord is near.

Malachi - 433 BC
Repentance and reformation as the prescription to cure the spirit of skepticism and indifference. Chastisement over tithes and offerings.

Student Notes:

About the Author

Raised in a relatively conservative Christian home, Margie Smith found the truths of Christ easy to accept. As a youth she personalized these truths and was baptisted, joining a Southern Baptist Church in Spokane, Washington. In college she and her husband Brian attended a rather unconventional Free Evangelical church, attending a weekly couples Bible study and working in the Baptist Student Ministries on campus.

In 1987 Margie and Brian moved to Dallas, Texas with their two children. Margie has been a life-long student of the Bible, teaching various children and adult Bible classes along the way. She has served as both a Small Group Leader and Coach in her current church, The Village, in Highland Village, Texas. Additionally, she owns a Dallas-based advertising agency.

Margie has always enjoyed working with new believers. She developed the Basic Bible 101 curriculum as a way to bridge the gap when adults become believers in Christ and attempt to understand the Bible for the first time in their lives.

Answers to the Homework and Lesson Notes
Answers to the questions posed in the homework and lesson notes can be found online at http://www.basicbible101.com under the Lesson Notes heading.

Quizzes, Handouts, Review Sheets and The Final Exam
To access the quizzes, handouts, review sheets and the final exam, log into the student area of the website using **student** as the username and **basicbible101** as the password.

How to Order More Workbooks
Basic Bible 101 Old Testament student workbooks can be purchased online through the Basic Bible 101 website (http://www.basicbible101.com) or you can write to:

Basic Bible 101
c/o Margie Smith
PO Box 941843
Plano, TX 75094

Email: margie@basicbible101.com

A New Testament version of this course is also available.

Made in the USA
Middletown, DE
21 September 2018